I Have Some Questions About God

Bradley Shavit Artson
Ed Feinstein • Elyse Frishman
Josh Hammerman
Jeff Salkin • Sybil Sheridan

Edited by Joel Lurie Grishaver

Illustrations by Michelle Noiset

We wish to thank
Debi Rowe, Micha'el Akiba
and Steven Starkman
who worked with us and offered
invaluable insights on this project.

Illustrations Copyright © 2002 Michelle Noiset

Credits

PAGE 51 (PHOTOGRAPH) © DAVE BARTRUFF/CORBIS

PAGES 80 (MIRIAM, ISAIAH, SOLOMON) AND 82 (RUTH & NATHAN) © STEPHEN SCHILDBACH

PAGES 3, 14, 15, 16, 22, 24, 32, 33, 44, 52,59, 60, 71, 81, 90, 91, 101, 109 AND 110 © EYEWIRE.COM

ISBN #1-891662-15-5

Torah Aura Productions• 4423 Fruitland Avenue, Los Angeles, CA 90058
(800) BE-Torah • (800) 238-6724 • (323) 585-7312 • fax (323) 585–0327
E-MAIL <misrad@torahaura.com>
Visit the Torah Aura website at www.torahaura.com

MANUFACTURED IN MALAYSIA THIRD PRINTING

Table of Contents

I Have Some Questions about God

I have a friend named Ben. Ben does not believe in God, but God is one of Ben's favorite subjects. Ben argues about God all the time. He spends a lot of time trying to prove to me that there is no God. I spend a lot of time trying to prove to him that there is a God. Neither of us will ever win. There is nothing I can say that will prove to him that there is a God, and there is nothing he can say to me that will make me doubt that there is a God.

I have no mathematical equation that I can write on a blackboard to prove that God is real. I can't take Ben to a museum and show him some ancient artifact on which he can use a magnifying glass to see God's fingerprints. I can only tell Ben my feelings and my thoughts.

There is nothing Ben can mix in a test tube that will prove to me that there is no God. He cannot open up a history book and show me a fact or a story that will get me to stop believing that God is here. All Ben can do is tell me why he doubts that there is a God and he can ask me questions about God that he thinks I can't answer.

Ben doesn't know that I have lots of questions about God, too. Everyone does.

If you believe in God—you have questions about God.

If you don't believe in God—you have questions about God.

And if you are not sure—then you, too, have questions about God.

This book is a collection of twelve questions about God that we collected from lots of kids. We asked oodles of kids for their questions about God and these were the most popular. Then we went to six rabbis in England and America and invited them to answer the questions. Most of their answers are stories. Most of the time they have different answers.

This book is a collection of their best answers to your questions. Read, enjoy, question, and join the discussion.

Joel Lurie Grishaver

What questions do you have about God?

How Do We Know
There Really Is A God?

Answer One: Rabbi Sybil Sheridan

The Garden in the Middle of the Forest

Two explorers were hacking through miles of undergrowth in a rain forest in the middle of nowhere. They came across a garden. "How amazing!" said one. "Just look at all this beauty. The trees are evenly spaced. There are flowers everywhere. And all of it is covered by the peaceful sound of splashing water."

"How can such a garden exist in the middle of a jungle?" asked the other.

The first answered, "It means we are near civilization. There is probably a palace around here. If we walk on a bit, we'll come to a town."

So the two walked on, but there was no sign of a palace or a town.

"This garden is a miracle," said the first explorer.

"No, it's not," replied the second, "some wealthy ruler has decided to plant a garden a long way away for real peace and quiet. If we wait here long enough, he will come to enjoy it."

So the two men waited, but no rich ruler came.

"Gardeners!" exclaimed the second explorer after a time, "There must be gardeners. Look at the design, the straight lines of the flowerbeds. There is not a weed in sight. If we wait here long enough, we will meet the gardeners and we can ask them where the garden came from."

They waited in the garden. They watched the seasons change. Flowers withered and faded, to be replaced with new young blooms. The trees flowered and bore fruit and then dropped their leaves. The leaves blew away, leaving the garden as neat and as beautiful as before. For months they waited in the garden, but no one came.

"There is no gardener. The garden is just a miracle," announced the first explorer.

"Maybe, the gardener comes at night while we are asleep. Perhaps, we should take turns watching through the night for him," said the second.

So they watched all night and all day. The flowers continued to bloom and fade. The trees budded and burst into flower. All year they waited in the garden, but no one came.

"Perhaps," said the second explorer, "the gardener is invisible. That would explain why we have seen no one at all."

"And perhaps there is no gardener. The garden just grew this way on its own."

They sat and watched the garden. And after a long, long time they said together, "We will never know."

The truth is, we can't know for certain if there really is a God. We can only guess that there is a God by picking up clues left around the world for us to find. Just because you can't see or touch something doesn't mean it isn't there. You can't see electricity, but you can see what it does. You can't touch oxygen, but without it you would die. Look around the universe and you can see God working, keeping it all going for us to enjoy.

Answer Two: Rabbi Ed Feinstein

I Just Have to Care

A man once came to a <u>H</u>asidic rabbi named Mena<u>h</u>em Mendel of Kotsk to complain. He said to him, "Rabbi, so many bad things happen in the world. I can't believe in God any more!"

The rabbi listened and said, "Why do you care?"

This surprised the man. "What do you mean, why do I care? It hurts me to see people hungry, sick and suffering. How could I not care?"

But the rabbi asked him again, "Why do you care?"

The man, now very angry, tried to answer, "Rabbi, it makes me angry to see a world filled with war and disease and hunger. Why must people suffer?"

The rabbi shook his head and asked again, "Why do you care?"

Now the man was really mad. He shouted at the rabbi, "I care, Rabbi, that's all, I just care. I have to care. I just can't stand by and watch people suffer! I'm a human being, and I care."

"Good," said the rabbi, "And as long as you care, we know God is real."

As long as we care, we know God is real.

Answer Three: Rabbi Jeff Salkin

Uh-Oh

One sign there is a God is the "Uh-oh! feeling." If you have ever done something wrong (or something that you thought might be wrong), you can often hear that little voice inside you saying that it is wrong. We call that voice "conscience." Now, no one is really sure where the conscience comes from. I would say that God is the source of the conscience.

God gives us that quiet voice that says "Uh-oh."

Answer 4: Aaron Roth

The Puppy

I didn't used to believe in God. I thought that science explained everything. Then one night, my father brought home a puppy. It was a purebred Golden Retriever pup, a girl, just six weeks old. Along with the rest of my family, I instantly fell in love with this fur ball we now know as Nelly. That got me thinking about the idea of love. Until that moment I believed that love was nothing more than a change in the chemical balance in the brain that made us feel pleasure and affection. But for some reason, after Nelly licked me, I started to think of the ability to love as a privilege, a gift. Love is probably the most significant reason I turned back to God. That is not to say that I never loved until that moment, far from it. I just started to think of it differently and started to do it more. Love can't be an accident.

Aaron Roth is seventeen years old and he went from not believing in God to believing in God. For Aaron, love was the proof that God exists. The feeling of love is so powerful that it had to have been created out of love—God's love.

Your Turn

How do you know there is a God? Is one of these answers close to your answer?

Rabbi Sybil Sheridan's story **The Garden in the Middle of the Forest:** The world we live in is like a perfect garden growing in the middle of the forest. We cannot figure out how it got there and we cannot see the force that created it. The garden seems too perfect to be an accident, but we just don't know. We can never be sure about God.

Rabbi Ed Feinstein's story **I Just Have to Care:** A man tells his Rabbi that he cannot believe in God because too many people are sick or hungry or suffer in other ways. His rabbi tells him the fact that he cares proves there is a God. Caring about other people is a gift from God.

Rabbi Jeff Salkin's belief that the **Uh-Oh** feeling is a sign: Different things give us hints that there is a God. One of them is the fact that people have a conscience.

Aaron Roth's story of falling in love with **The Puppy:** He knew that love could not be an accident. Love has to be a gift from a loving God.

Do you have another reason for believing that there is a God?

hide and seek

Many different rabbis have told this story. A boy is playing hide-and-seek. The boy hides so well that his friends give up and go home. Still the boy hides for a long time, waiting to be found. After a long time he runs to his grandfather in tears. He says, "I was hiding and no one was seeking. They stopped looking for me." His grandfather hugged the boy and said, "God says exactly the same thing. "I am hiding and they stopped looking for me."

1. Why do you think that God is hidden and hard to find?

   Because he dosn't want any one to see him.

2. In which of these places can you get a glimpse that God is present?

   _____ A beautiful sunset   _____ A Hebrew school classroom

   _____ A mother with a newborn child   _____ Two best friends talking

   _____ Someone feeding a hungry person _____ An artist making a painting

   _____ Neighbors arguing   _____ An Olympic record being broken

   _____ A class cleaning a polluted stream _____ A family having a Shabbat dinner

3. Name two other places where you can see a clue that God is around.

   _____

   _____

Eli Eli

Hannah Szenes (Senesh) was a Jewish spy who tried to help Jews escape from Poland during World War II. She was not religious, but she wrote a poem. "Eli, Eli."

My God, My God,

I pray that these things never end:

The sand and the sea,

The rush of the waters,

The thunder of heaven,

Human prayers.

Hannah Szenes, written in Caesarea, near Kibbutz Sdot Yam, 1942.

1. Why would someone who did not go to services or observe most religious customs write a poem about God?

_____

_____

2. What else would you put on a list of things that you hope will never end?

_____

_____

_____

There is a famous mitzvah (commandment) in the Torah:

You must love the Eternal your God

Deuteronomy 6.5

Rashi was a famous biblical commentator. He had a lot of problems with this commandment. Rashi said, "It is impossible to command love. Love is something that grows." Rashi then explained, "What God actually wants us to do is to follow the mitzvot in the Torah—these are things that show love." Through doing these things we will come to know and love God.

Loving God Through Actions

Here are some mitzvot. In what way does each of these demonstrate love?

a. Saying the Shema at bedtime

b. Eating matzah during Passover

c. Helping a poor person

d. Taking care of the environment

e. Celebrating Shabbat

f. Studying Torah

g. Respecting the elderly

h. Not cheating at business

What are some other things you should do to show your love for God?

_____

_____

_____

16

Where Does God Come From?

Answer One: Rabbi Brad Artson

A Lesson from Monique

I am an *abba*. *Abba* is Hebrew for "Daddy." I have two children, Shira and Jacob. Since they are twins, they are both the same age—six years old. This is a story about Shira. It's also a story about things that fall apart and things that last forever.

Shira and I were visiting at her Mama's house (that's what she calls her grandmother, my mother). She was opening up Mama's drawers, looking through her cabinets, and exploring her house. We were on a treasure hunt. At the bottom of one closet, Shira discovered an old shoebox. Inside, she found a stuffed doll, a cat. The cat looked very old and very used. Her tail stuffing was long gone. One eye had popped off, and her belly was open at the top. Shira had discovered the doll that I slept with every night when I was a baby and a little boy.

Looking at the doll for the first time in thirty-five years, I could feel the same feelings of love I had when I was a child. But now, as a grown up, I could also see that Monique (that was the name I gave the doll when I first got it) was falling apart. Dolls don't last forever. They are made of cloth and stuffing and thread. Dolls, like everything you can touch, wear out over time. Monique was pretty close to being unusable.

When she was new, she was a beautiful doll. When they first brought her home, her eyes were shiny black, her fur was soft and fluffy, and she had a music box inside her belly that played a pretty song. Whoever made her had done a good job. But that was a long time ago, and her body wouldn't last much longer. But the feelings she had stirred in me weren't physical. Feelings like love and joy and connection don't have to have an end, and they don't have to have a beginning either. They just go on and on and on.

Shira took the doll out of the box and asked, "Abba, what is this?" I told her that the doll used to be my doll when I was a little boy and that her name was Monique. Shira looked at me, looked at Monique, and then held it to her chest. "Abba, now Monique is ours. We can both share her." Shira was able to see past the physical Monique, the part that would fall apart. She was able to feel what I felt. She could make that doll a way of connecting to the love she and I have for each other. Shira has slept with Monique every night since that visit to Mama's house.

People are born at a particular time. But thoughts, feelings and joy don't have a beginning or an end. Like my feelings for Monique, they can be passed from one person to another. The source of those feelings is God. God doesn't have a beginning or an end. God doesn't come from anywhere. God always was and always will be.

Answer Two: Rabbi Sybil Sheridan
and Rabbi Jeff Salkin

God is Forever

Many of our rabbis gave the same answer to this question. Here are two answers that are more or less the same.

There has always been God, but there haven't always been places "to come from." God was around even before there was a "here." It doesn't matter if your best friend comes from New York or Nebraska. What matters is the kind of person he or she is. It's the same with God. It doesn't matter where God is. It could be that God is outside outer space and looking down on the world. It could be that God is inside each of us. *What matters is what God does for us and what we can do for God.*

Rabbi Sybil Sheridan

Nowhere. God comes from nowhere. God is everywhere. God has always been around. God will always be around. God has no start. God has no end. *It's hard to imagine, but it's true.*

Rabbi Jeff Salkin

Your Turn

Where does God come from?

This is a question we love to ask but the answers we get are not simple. God does not come from Cleveland or Baltimore. God does not come from Mars or Pluto or the Ring Nebula. There was "No Thing" before God who gave birth to God.

Rabbi Artson had a doll named Monique that he loved when he was very young. Later, his daughter Shira found and also loved Monique. The feeling of love was passed from one person to another. Rabbi Artson explains that God is like a feeling. Feelings don't have beginnings. Feelings, like love for a doll, are things that can be passed on and on.

Both Rabbi Salkin and Rabbi Sheridan said, "God doesn't have a beginning. God is forever." Even though that is hard to imagine, that is one of the things that makes God different from the things that God created.

Where do you think God came from?

All three of our rabbis said "God didn't come from anywhere." Do you have your own way of explaining this?

The Letter Bet Teaches Us A Lesson

בּ is Bet. Bet is the first letter in the Torah. It starts the word בְּרֵאשִׁית Bereshit, beginnings.

The Rabbis asked, "Why does the Torah begin with a Bet?" One of the answers they gave was this, "The Bet is closed on three sides. We will never know what is above us in heaven. We will never understand what is below us. We will never know what came before creation, because the Bet is closed to the past too. The only open side is the future. We can help plan and create the future."

Zohar, Bahir

The Bet has a foot that is pointed back toward the Alef. That teaches us that God was before creation—God was before anything else.

Malbim

Lamed is the last letter
in the Torah. Make up
your own lesson about
God based on the shape
of the Lamed.

23

WHERE DID YOU COME FROM?

The Talmud teaches that there were three partners in your creation: your mother, your father and God.

List three things you got from a parent

_____
_____
_____
_____

List three things you got from another adult

_____
_____
_____
_____

List three things you got from God.

_____
_____
_____
_____

If There Is One God, Why Are There So Many Religions?

Answer One: Rabbi Sybil Sheridan

The Blindfolded Children and the Elephant

ive children were blindfolded and put in a room with an elephant and asked to describe it. But none of them had ever seen an elephant.

"Hey folks!" cried one kid, grabbing hold of its trunk, "This elephant is just like a huge snake."

"Don't be silly," said another, holding its tail, "It's not that big; it's more like a large worm."

26

"What are you talking about?" joined in a third, with arms around one of the elephant's legs. "This elephant is as big and as strong as a tree trunk."

"More like a tent," announced the fourth child, who was standing underneath the elephant stroking its belly.

"It's too hard for a tent," said the last, feeling the tusk, "It has a giant shell—it must be like some kind of great mollusk."

Which child was right? If they had been asked to draw the elephant, would they have been able to do so?

In fact, every one of them was right. An elephant's trunk is rather like a snake; its tusks are like mollusks; its tail a worm; its hide like a tent; and its legs are as big as tree trunks. But these kids only had part of the elephant to feel, and without seeing the whole of it they could not picture what it really was. A whole elephant is much more than just those parts.

This is our problem with God. No one has actually seen all of God, though many people have glimpsed little bits. We make up our whole picture of God from the little bits we know. That is why there are so many different religions, because all our pictures are so different. Probably not one of them is completely right, though like our elephant, there are bits of truth in them all.

Finding God is like a treasure hunt: Everyone on the hunt will have a different way of going about it. We may even start from different places on the map. Some will look for clues to find God in the world around us, others in what has happened in our history, while still others look for clues in the sacred texts of our faith. Wherever we look, we are likely to find some of the answers but not all of them. Every religion has found some of the clues. They may be different than yours, but they all point to the same God, waiting to be found.

Answer Two: Rabbi Jeff Salkin

Finding God is Like Cimbing a Mountain

I got this idea from my friends, Rabbi Marc Gellman and Father Tom Hartman.

Imagine that God is at the top of a mountain. Many different groups want to be close to God. But each group has its own map for climbing the mountain—Jews, Christians, Muslims, Hindus, and many other groups. Each group climbs up the mountain on their own path. Sometimes the paths cross, and you can actually wave to the other people who are climbing the mountain.

God likes the idea that there are many different maps to get up the mountain. God wants the different groups of climbers to be kind to each other, and sometimes even to learn from each other.

Answer Three: Joel Lurie Grishaver

In the Beginning There Was One Religion

In the beginning there were just two people, Adam and Eve, and one God. Religion was pretty simple—Adam and Eve talked to God. But there was also a problem. God gave the two people one mitzvah, "Don't touch the tree in the middle of the garden." Eve and Adam messed up. From then on, there was a distance between people and God. People's feelings sometimes led them to do what they wanted, rather than what God wanted. Things got worse and worse, until God hated everything and sent a flood so that the world could start over. After the flood, God felt badly and promised, "No more floods." God gave people seven rules that everyone had to follow. These rules were a contract between all people and God. These rules, Noah's family's seven commandments, are at the heart of every religion. However, these rules didn't work well enough. Too often, people still did what they wanted and not what was right. God got frustrated and needed a new answer. So God picked Sarah and Abraham's family and used them as an experiment. God gave Abraham and Sara's family the Torah, with 613 mitzvot (commandments). God planned it so that once they learned how to control their behavior and live up to God's expectations, God could then use their success to teach everyone else. The Jewish people chose to be part of this experiment and follow the rules in the Torah. This commitment makes us "The Choosing People."

Your Turn

It is so confusing to have so many different religions. It would be much easier if everyone could just believe and do the same things. But, that is not the way the world is.

If there is only one God, why are their so many different religions?

Rabbi Sheridan told the story of **The Blindfolded Children and the Elephant.** She said that God is so big that each of us can see only a small part of God. Different religions come from the different ways each of us knows God.

Rabbi Salkin said that finding God is like climbing a mountain. There are many different ways up the mountain. Each religion is a different path, but they are all aiming toward the same God.

Joel Grishaver told the story, **In the Beginning There Was One Religion.** It is the story of Eve and Adam, Noah, and Sarah and Abraham. God is working on ways to help people control their behavior and be the best people they can be. Judaism is one of God's experiments, a way of helping people learn how to be better people.

Is one of these explanations close to your understanding?

Do you have a different way of explaining why there are so many religions?

Finding Your Torah

The rabbis teach that every person has his or her own Torah. This means that every person has his or her own piece of the total wisdom that there is for people to learn.

Rabbi Yehudah Aryeh Leib Alter, a rabbi known as the S'fat Emet taught, "The entire Torah was given to the Jewish people as a whole. However, each person has his or her own particular teaching, a specific goal for his or her life."

For the S'fat Emet, the total Torah is more than the words on the scroll. It is more like a jigsaw puzzle. God gave one piece to each person. Our job is to gather Torah from everyone we meet—and make the whole Torah larger and larger.

Here are two examples of people who have taught me pieces of wisdom I will treasure forever.

The Person	The Person's Torah
My Uncle Seymour 	My Uncle Seymour had cerebral palsy. It damaged his whole body. It made it difficult for him to walk and even talk. He refused to use a wheel chair and he walked with the help of canes. He became a lawyer. He spent his whole life finding ways of doing things that seemrf impossible. My Uncle Seymour's Torah was that God gives us as much strength as we need.
My Neighbor Mary 	I live in an apartment building made of brick and steel and it is kind of old. My neighbor Mary loves plants. She grows them in her apartment, on the balconies and the outside staircases. Our building is now green, and there are flowers all over. Mary taught me that God gives us the wisdom to make life grow almost everywhere.

Name three people who have taught you a piece of wisdom.

The Person   The Person's Torah

_____   _____

                            _____

                            _____

_____   _____

                            _____

                            _____

                            _____

_____   _____

                            _____

Noah's Family's Seven Commandments

We learn in a midrash that God gave Adam six mitzvot that Adam and Eve were supposed to follow. God then added one more mitzvah for Noah's family. That completed Noah's family's seven mitzvot. Imagine what these seven rules would be. Make up your own list of seven commandments that every person should follow. These should be seven rules that are at the heart of all religions. Make up your own list on this page, and then compare it to the list of the commandments God gave to Noah on the following page.

1._____

2._____

3._____

4._____

5._____

6._____

7._____

Noah's Family's Seven Commandments

This is the list of commandments the Midrash tells us were given to Noah's family.

1. There must be rules and judges to make sure that everyone is treated fairly.

2. Everyone must know that one God created all people and all things.

3. No one should worship idols or think that a thing made by a person could be considered a god.

4. No one can murder or intentionally injure anyone else.

5. Families must be protected and considered holy.

6. No one can steal.

7. No one should be cruel to animals.

For discussion:

a. How many of the commandments on God's list were on your list?

b. Do any of God's commandments surprise you?

c. Try to figure out why the ones that surprise you are on the list.

Does God Know What I Am Thinking or What I Will Do?

Answer One: Rabbi Elyse Frishman

Adam and Eve Were Not Robots

magine how beautiful it was in the Garden of Eden. If you turned in any direction you would see long-stemmed flowers of every color, butterflies flitting from one flower to the next, soft green grass, trees full with delicious fruit. When the sun got too hot, you could sit under any tree. You could feel the cool shade, rest your back against the strong trunk of a tree. You could just lift up your hand and pluck off a perfect apple or pear, apricot or orange, date or fig. If you took one big bite, you'd fill your mouth with the best flavor, and the juice would run down your chin. Yum!

Adam was the only person around and he was lonely. While he fell asleep one night, God magically made Eve from his side. And when he awoke in the morning, Adam was happier than he had ever been.

In the middle of the Garden of Eden were two mysterious trees. They looked like fig trees, but God called them by different names. God said, "This one is the Tree of Knowledge of Good and Evil; and this one is the Tree of Life." God had told Adam not to eat the fruit of the Tree of Knowledge. After Eve was created, Adam told this to her.

Once, Eve was standing near the Tree of Knowledge, and a serpent appeared and told her, "You might want to eat this fruit. It will make you wise." Eve thought about this. She remembered what Adam had told her. She looked at those figs, and saw how delicious they looked. What really made her want to taste them? She thought to herself, "Wisdom? That sounds like something good to have." She reached up and broke off two figs, bit into one, and gave the other to Adam to eat.

Well, lo and behold, their eyes were opened. It was like a light bulb going on above a cartoon person's head! They could really think and understand things like never before. They were excited and happy. Then, it occurred to them, "Uh oh, God might be mad at us." And so they hid.

Now, can you really and truly hide from God? No way! God isn't like a human being who can only do certain things. God can do anything—and God knew what was going on in the Garden of Eden.

Did God know that Adam and Eve would eat from the Tree of Knowledge *before* they did? That we don't know. But we *do* know that after they ate the fruit of the Tree of Knowledge, Adam and Eve could sense God all around them. God had always been there, but they hadn't realized it. It was as if they had been blind to color, or deaf to sound. Suddenly they were given the power to see or hear. Once they ate the fruit, they could feel God everywhere.

Adam and Eve were freaked out. Both of them did the same thing—they hid from God. How? By pretending that God wasn't there. It was like when you're in your room playing, and you don't want to be bothered when your Mom calls you. You pretend that you didn't hear—and in a way, you really didn't.

That's exactly what Adam and Eve did. God was really upset. Maybe God was even lonely. So God cried out, sad and angry at the same time, "Where are you guys?" And Adam answered, "I was afraid of You, God, so I hid."

What do we learn from this story? God decided that people would not be robots. God let us have freedom and allowed us to think for ourselves. For us to have freedom, God can't know exactly what's going to happen next.

It's like keeping a diary and not wanting your parent to read it. You tell all your secrets to your diary. You leave it in your room in the top drawer of your desk. Now, the truth is, if your Mom or Dad wanted to read it, they probably could. But do they? No. They understand that it is important for you to have your privacy. They choose to let you have freedom. They choose not to find out everything that's going on in your life. That is exactly what God does. It takes a lot of love and trust to let someone have freedom.

Answer Two: Rabbi Ed Feinstein

God's Voice is Inside Us

Remember the story of Moses at the burning bush? Suppose you were making a movie of that story. What would God's voice sound like? Would you choose a loud, deep voice like Darth Vader's? Or a soft voice? A man's voice or a woman's voice? Some rabbis once asked this, and they decided that when God spoke to Moses from out of the bush, God spoke in Moses' own voice.

When do we hear our own voice? When we think about what's right and what's wrong we often hear a voice inside us telling us which way to go. When that happens we hear our own voice. When I see someone who is sick or lonely or hurting, and I wonder if I should go help, I hear my own voice telling me what to do. According to the rabbis, that's the same voice Moses heard at the burning bush.

God is inside us, not like someone spying on our thoughts but like someone helping us decide the right thing to do. God can't force us to do what's right, but God can remind us to care.

Answer Three: Rabbi Joshua Hammerman

God Lights the Spark

When we are inspired to think a new thought, or when we are moved to help someone in need, it is God who inspires us. God is the spark that sets off the thought, but we are free to think in our own way and act as we wish. God doesn't guide our every action, but in the big picture, I do feel that God sets a direction for each of us. We were created with enough "God DNA" within us to give us the potential to choose to do good.

Usually it is only after the fact that we reflect on something we've done or an idea we've had and we think, "God must have wanted us to do it this way."

40

Your Turn

Three of our rabbis gave us very different ways of thinking
about whether God knows our thoughts and controls our actions.

Adam and Eve Were Not Robots: Rabbi Elyse Frishman taught us that when Adam and Eve were first created, God allowed them to do the wrong thing. God did not control them and God does not control us. Rabbi Frishman taught that God is like our parents with our diary. Even if our parents could find and read our diary, they respect our privacy and don't open the book. God is the same way with our thoughts.

God's Voice Is Inside Us: Rabbi Ed Feinstein taught us that a midrash says that when Moses heard God at the burning bush, God used Moses' own voice to talk to him. We hear God's voice inside us all the time. It coaches us to do the best we can, and it warns us when we are going to do the wrong thing. A coach helps us know what to do but does not control our actions.

God Lights the Spark: Rabbi Joshua Hammerman teaches us that when we get a great idea or suddenly have an insight, God is at work. God helps us to understand the world but does not control what we do.

Does one of these three answers make sense to you?
Does God know our thoughts or control our actions? What is your answer?

How Do We Know What God Is Thinking?

The other side of the question, "Does God know what we are thinking?" is "Can we know what God is thinking?" The other side of the question, "Does God control what we do?" is "Can we let God help us know the right thing to do?"

The Action	Have you done it?	Has it helped you to understand God?	Has it helped you to know what to do?
1. Praying in Synagogue	_____	_____	_____
2. Meditating	_____	_____	_____
3. Talking to God	_____	_____	_____
4. Studying Torah	_____	_____	_____
5. Reading a Book	_____	_____	_____

The Action	Have you done it?	Has it helped you to understand God?	Has it helped you to know what to do?
6. Studying With a Friend	_____	_____	_____
7. Giving Charity	_____	_____	_____
8. Dancing	_____	_____	_____
9. Singing	_____	_____	_____
10. Creating Art	_____	_____	_____

In Judaism, there are many ways of getting closer to God
and knowing what God wants.

Jewish Laws Of Privacy

Balaam was a wizard who was hired to put a curse on Israel. He went up to the top of a mountain and raised his hands. Then something changed his mind. The words that were supposed to be a curse came out as a blessing. The curse came out as,

"Your tents are really good Israel; so are the places where you live, Jacob."

The rabbis of long ago were really curious about what turned the curse into a blessing. One of their answers had to do with the way Israel's tents were set up. Israel had carefully turned each tent so that no one could look into another person's dwelling place. Balaam was impressed with their respect for privacy.

Jews have many rules about privacy. Here are a few.

- The Talmud says that a person should knock before opening a closed door, even in his or her own house.

- The Talmud also teaches that you may not put a window in the wall of your house if it looks in on someone else's house.

- Rabbi Gershom ben Yehudah Me'or HaGolah made it a rule that no one may open or read anyone else's mail.

Write three of your own privacy rules.

1. _____

2. _____

3. _____

How is respecting privacy a way of getting closer to God?

_____

_____

_____

Can Praying
Make Someone Well?

Answer One: Rabbi Ed Feinstein
The Way to Paradise

There was a man who gave up on life. He found no joy in his work, family or friends. So he prayed to God to show him the way to Paradise. God showed him. And it turned out that Paradise wasn't very far. One afternoon, he set out. He walked until nightfall and then decided to rest beneath a leafy tree. Just before he fell asleep, it occurred to him that in the morning he might become confused and forget the way to Paradise. So he left his shoes by the roadside, pointing toward Paradise. All he had to do in the morning was jump in the shoes and continue walking.

But sometimes, things happen in life. While he slept, the man's shoes got turned around. Was it an imp? an angel? a squirrel? In the morning, the man rose and continued his journey, unaware that he was returning home.

By noon, he spotted a village on the next hillside, and his heart leapt, "I've arrived, it's Paradise!" He ran up the hill until he arrived in the town.

Sitting in the town square, he fell in love with Paradise. He heard the songs of children in school, and the laughter of adults at work. For the first time in his life, he felt the energy and love that filled the village. All day, he sat in the square and listened.

By nighttime, he began to feel hungry. "Since Paradise looks so much like my town," he thought, "I wonder if there is a street in Paradise like my street?" He looked and found it just where he thought it might be.

"I wonder if there is a house in Paradise like my house?" And there it was. Just as he was admiring this house, a woman came to the door—a woman who looked just like his wife. She called his name and told him to come in for dinner. "They know me in Paradise! There is a place set for me here in Paradise!"

The house here in Paradise was not like his house. That house was crowded and noisy. This place was cozy and filled with life. He sat and ate the best meal he'd ever eaten. And afterwards, he slept the deepest, most restful sleep he'd ever known.

In the morning, the woman who looked like his wife handed him his tools and sent him to work. Work? But of course, even in Paradise there are tasks. But this work was different than the man's work at home. This was filled with a sense of purpose and service. And that night, he returned to that warm and loving home.

Do you know, that old fool never learned that he hadn't really made it to Paradise, because every day was better than the day before.

God doesn't make us sick. We get sick because we have bodies, and our bodies are vulnerable to germs and viruses and injuries. And when our bodies get sick, God doesn't make our bodies get better. Resting, eating and drinking right and taking medicine help our bodies heal and get better. What does God do? God turns our shoes around. God can change our attitude. God can strengthen our desire to get better, our will to fight the disease. God can keep us from giving up. God can help us learn from being sick, teaching us that health is a precious gift. God can help us remember that each day is special and that even here and now, we can find Paradise.

Answer Two: Rabbi Joshua Hammerman

God Lights the Fire

Praying brings God into our thoughts and actions. It's like rubbing two sticks together to create a fire. Sometimes it works, especially if others are doing the same thing and helping you out. At other times, the sticks are too wet or the time is just not right. But even then, by rubbing the sticks together, we stay in practice and help to dry out the kindling so that perhaps the next time it will "take."

Once we ignite that spark and bring God into our lives, there is a sense of healing within us that can help us get better when we are ill; and it can help others to set off the same spark within them. Prayer can do all that, but not every time.

Answer Three:
Rabbi Elyse Frishman

Praying With Our Feet

A famous Jew named Abraham Joshua Heschel once said that you can pray with your feet. He meant that when you walk to help someone in need, you are praying. He also taught that prayer does not necessarily change the world around us. Prayer does not make sick people well or stop wars or keep earthquakes from happening. But prayer does make you strong enough to handle any situation; it gives you courage and helps you not be afraid.

When we are sad or lonely or hurt or scared and someone helps us, that is like God hugging us. When we touch other people with loving hands, when we help people who are sad or hungry or lonely or scared, we are bringing God to them.

When sick people know you are praying for them, it makes them feel better. And our minds can help our bodies to get better, too.

49

Your Turn

All three of our Rabbis thought that prayers to God could help you get well when you are sick. However, all three of them thought about God's help in a different way.

Rabbi Feinstein told the story, **The Way to Paradise.** It is the story of a man who is unhappy, so he sets off for Paradise and falls alseep half way there. In the middle of the night his shoes get turned around so that he winds up going home and thinking that it is Paradise. Rabbi Feinstein says, "God does not make us sick; our bodies get sick. God does not make us well; our bodies get better. But, God can turn our shoes around and help us to see the world differently, and that can help us get better."

Rabbi Hammerman said something similar to Rabbi Feinstein. He said, "God lights the fire." He said that praying is like lighting a fire. That fire is the warmth of God being close. When God feels closer, it sometimes makes us feel better.

Rabbi Frishman had a completely different idea. She taught about "praying with our feet." She told us about a lesson from Rabbi Abraham Joshua Heschel, who said that people can pray with words or with actions. When we visit people who are sick, or when we help then in other ways, we are saying prayers that can help them get better.

Is one of these ideas close to your answer to the question?
Do you have a different way of understanding how God helps us get well when we are sick?

A Prayer for Healing

Traditionally during the Torah service, we say a prayer called *Mi She-Berakh*. It is a prayer that asks God to help the sick people we know to get well. During the *Mi She-Berakh* we name or think of specific people.

MAY GOD WHO BLESSED
OUR ANCESTORS,
ABRAHAM, ISAAC AND JACOB,
SARAH, REBEKKAH, RACHEL AND LEAH,
BLESS AND HEAL _____.
MAY THE HOLY ONE IN MERCY
ON HIM OR HER
STRENGTHEN AND HEAL,
AND SEND A SPEEDY RECOVERY,
IN BODY AND SOUL,
TOGETHER WITH OTHERS
WHO SUFFER ILLNESS.
AND LET US SAY…AMEN.

Debbie Friedman took the words of the *Mi She-Berakh* and wrote a song. Do you know it?

Write your own healing prayer. What words would you use to ask God to help someone you know or someone you love to get better?

_____

_____

_____

VISITING THE SICK

The mitzvah of visiting the sick is called bikkur <u>h</u>olim. We believe that when we visit the sick we are being like God, helping people to get well.

A student of Rabbi Akiva was once very sick, and no one came to see him. So as soon as Rabbi Akiva heard, he went and visited his student. When Rabbi Akiva got there he saw that the student's room was a mess. Rabbi Akiva cleaned as he visited. He even scrubbed the floor. The student got well. Afterwards the student told everyone, "Rabbi Akiva's visit saved my life." (Nedarim 40b)

How did Rabbi Akiva's visit save his student's life?

_____

_____

_____

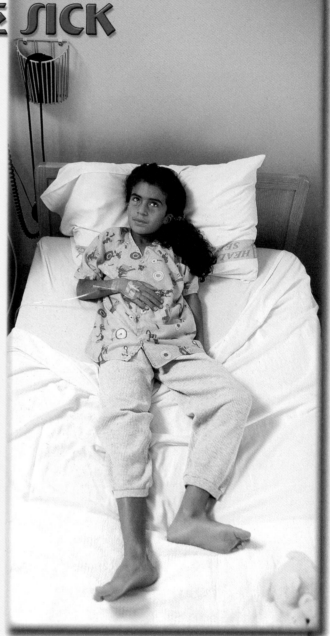

Write three rules about visiting people who are sick.

1. _____

2. _____

3. _____

Does God Care
Which Team Wins
The World Series
or The Super Bowl?

Answer One: Rabbi Joshua Hammerman

The Red Sox Blow the Pennant on Simhat Torah

God cares about sports because it's one way that God teaches us how to care.

As a young boy growing up near Boston, Massachusetts, I looked forward to two things every spring: Passover and opening day of baseball season. Two things that I loved more than anything were being with my family at the seders and being with 33,000 other Red Sox fans at Fenway Park.

Simhat Torah of 1986 came at the same time as a very famous World Series game. On Simhat Torah night, my beloved Boston Red Sox had blown the ultimate chance to win their first Series since 1918, losing the sixth game to the Mets in a heartbreaking fashion. I cried for half the night, wondering why God could allow this to happen. Then, the following morning, I caught myself crying again while dancing with the Torah.

At that point I stopped in my tracks. I wondered what I cared about more: a sports team or the Torah? For which one had people given their lives over the centuries? Which one had taught me how to live a good life? Which one had instilled people with hope during times much darker than these? I decided that it was time to stop crying over the Red Sox, and start rejoicing with the Torah.

But I also understood at that moment why sports are so important. My caring so deeply for the Red Sox is what taught me how care for the Torah and other important things. That caring taught me how to be a good loser and a gracious winner, how to sacrifice for the team and how to feel for the guy who had just struck out. That caring also helped me to understand how God feels about us and how painful it must be for God to watch when we strike out.

Loving the Red Sox has also helped me to love other people. If the love of a sports team can bring so many different types of people together, simply because they happen to live near the same city, that teaches us that we're not that different after all. For that reason, I believe that God does indeed care about who wins the World Series and the Super Bowl.

Answer Two: Rabbi Brad Artson

God Cares About Values

On the one hand, God doesn't care who wins the World Series, because it's just a game. There are no issues of justice, of righteousness or of kindness at stake. God cares about those values and about all the players whether they win or not.

But on the other hand, if winning is the result of teamwork, of learning cooperation and hard work, then I suppose those are things that would please God. God likes to see people become the best they can be.

There is a Jewish way to play baseball—one that involves learning fairness, participation and honesty. God cares about that.

Answer Three: Rabbi Elyse Frishman

God Likes Sandy Koufax

I think that one of God's favorite sports heroes must have been Sandy Koufax because he kept God's rule about Yom Kippur. This meant that he couldn't play in one of the World Series games. God's rules matter more than anyone else's rules, because God's rules are for the good of everyone.

God cares more about how we play the game than who wins.

57

Your Turn

Each of our rabbis gave us a different answer to the question about whether God cares about who wins The Super Bowl or The World Series in a different way.

 Rabbi Hammerman told the story of how the **Red Sox** taught him to really care about something. He said, "That caring taught me how to be a good loser and a gracious winner, how to sacrifice for the team and how to feel for the guy who had just struck out." He believes that God wants sports heroes to be good examples for us.

 Rabbi Artson said, "God does not care who wins", but God does care about how people play. He said, "There is a Jewish way to play baseball—one that involves learning fairness, participation and honesty."

 Rabbi Frishman told the story of **Sandy Koufax** who would not pitch in the World Series when the game was on Yom Kippur. Not playing on Yom Kippur is following a rule in the Torah. Rabbi Frishman said, "God's rules matter more than anyone else's rules, because God's rules are for the good of everyone."

Do you like any of these answers to the question?
Is one of them close to your answer? Do you have a different answer?

The Jewish way to Play

Rabbi Artson said, "There is a Jewish way to play baseball." That means that there is a Jewish way to play every sport. Here is a list of Jewish values. Mark all the ones that should be part of every game.

_____ **Anavah**—being humble

_____ **Dan l'khaf z'khut**—giving the benefit of the doubt

_____ **Emet**—being truthful

_____ **Erekh apayim**—controlling your temper

_____ **K'vod ha-briot**—honoring everyone

_____ **Lo l'vayesh**—not embarrassing anyone

_____ **Ometz lev**—being brave

_____ **Shmirat ha-guf**—taking care of your body

_____ **Shmirat ha-lashon**—watching your mouth

_____ **Yirat ha-shamayim**—remembering God

Which value do you think is most important? Which one do you think is the hardest to remember during a game?

59

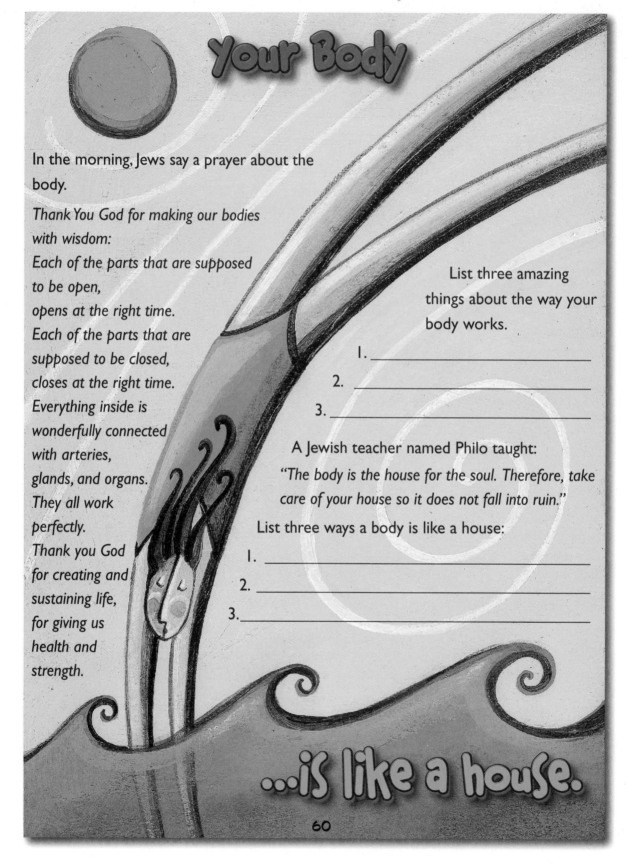

Your Body

In the morning, Jews say a prayer about the body.

Thank You God for making our bodies with wisdom:
Each of the parts that are supposed to be open,
opens at the right time.
Each of the parts that are supposed to be closed,
closes at the right time.
Everything inside is wonderfully connected with arteries,
glands, and organs.
They all work perfectly.
Thank you God for creating and sustaining life,
for giving us health and strength.

List three amazing things about the way your body works.

1. _____
2. _____
3. _____

A Jewish teacher named Philo taught:

"*The body is the house for the soul. Therefore, take care of your house so it does not fall into ruin.*"

List three ways a body is like a house:

1. _____
2. _____
3. _____

...is like a house.

Does God Understand Hebrew Best?

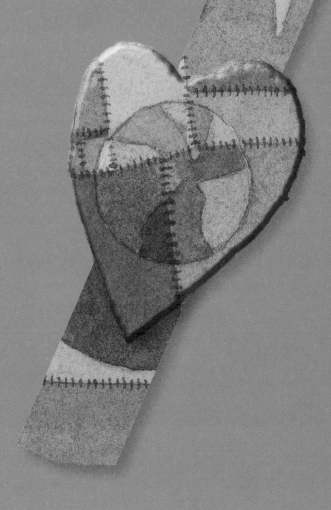

Answer One: Rabbi Elyse Frishman
The Story of the Flute

There was once a great teacher who was called the Baal Shem Tov. In his village there was a family with a son who had not learned how to read. His father was a shepherd. Every day the boy and his father would go out to the meadow to care for the sheep until sunset. The boy had a little wooden flute that his grandfather had carved for him. Each day he sat in the shade of his favorite tree, leaned his back against the strong trunk and tootled on the flute. At night he would sit outside his family's little hut and continue to play quietly to himself. So it was that the boy sang with his flute even more than he talked.

The only day that was really hard for the boy was Shabbat when he was not allowed to play an instrument. The little boy insisted on keeping the flute with him at all times, and that meant that the father could not allow the boy to join him in shul for Shabbat prayers. He was worried that the boy might start playing the flute, so the boy was left at home.

One year, as Rosh ha-Shanah drew closer and closer, the boy begged his father to let him come to shul. "Please Papa. I want so much to hear the shofar. I am old enough. Please, please bring me with you." Day after day he pleaded with his father until finally Papa agreed. "But only on the condition that you leave your flute at home!" Demanded the father.

It was the morning of Rosh Ha-Shanah and the boy was thrilled. He couldn't believe that he was going to hear the shofar, see the Torah and join all the other people in their songs and prayers to God. What an honor! He dressed quickly, and oops...he slipped the little flute into his pocket. Really, it was out of habit. He hadn't meant to disobey his father.

The boy and his father walked to shul hand in hand. They joined a hundred other people in the crowded and noisy sanctuary. The boy kept tugging his father's jacket, "Is it time for the shofar yet?" Time after time his father hushed him.

Soon, the service began. At the very front of the room, the boy could barely see the Baal Shem Tov, wrapped in his *tallit*, swaying back and forth as he sang the prayers. Sometimes the great leader would lift his arms up to heaven, as though he were begging God to listen.

Even as the singing and praying got more intense, the Baal Shem Tov wasn't very happy at all.

But the little boy didn't care. He was so happy to be there; he kept listeni ng to everyone praying. More than anything he wanted to join in, but he didn't know Hebrew, and he certainly didn't know how to read. So he had to be quiet. His hands kept going to the flute hidden in his pocket. His fingers touched the little holes in the flute, imagining the sounds that he would make if his lips were pressed to the opening of the flute. As the prayers grew more and more intense, the boy's desire grew to take out the flute and blow it. It was harder and harder for him not to take out the flute.

Then came the time for the blowing of the shofar. Oh, it was just as he had imagined! Everyone got completely quiet. The Baal Shem Tov lifted up the ram's horn and raised it high up so that it seemed to curve all the way to the heavens. He placed his mouth to the opening and blew the mightiest blasts ever heard. *Te'kiah! ah-ooo! Sh'varim! ah-ooo! ah-ooo! ah-ooo! T'ruah! oo! oo! oo! oo! oo! oo! oo! oo! oo!* After each of the blasts, everyone sang and stomped their feet.

It was too much for the boy. He couldn't sing. He didn't know any of the Hebrew words. He didn't understand anything. But he felt the power of what they were doing and wanted more than anything to join in.

Then it happened. The last blast of the shofar was being called. Everyone in the room was still and quiet as a mouse. His father had taught him that *T'kiah G'dolah*, the last call is the greatest of all. It is a long and mighty blast that could go on for several minutes. "*T'kiah g'dolaaaaaaaaaaaaaaaaaaaaaaaa…h*" the caller cried out, holding the last sound till his breath ran out. It was completely quiet for a moment. The Baal Shem Tov began to blow, gently at first, increasing in sound and strength, until....

No one saw the boy remove the flute from his pocket. All the people were either watching the Baal Shem Tov or had their eyes closed so they could listen carefully. Without think-ing, faster than a blink of the eye, the boy lifted the flute to his mouth and blew the loud-est, longest note that he could. You can imagine what happened next. His father shrieked, "What are you doing?" and grabbed the flute from his son. Everyone was frozen. All the people were shocked that this boy had interrupted the Baal Shem Tov in the middle of the *Tekiah Gedolah*. What did the Baal Shem Tov do? He stopped in the middle of that *Tekiah Gedolah*. Was he furious at this child who could not control himself? Was he angry that the father had let the boy bring his flute? Was he upset that the most important moment in the Rosh ha-Shanah service had been interrupted?

He put the shofar down and did something he'd never done before. He left the front of the room and walked all the way to the back where the boy was standing. The boy was not afraid. He lifted his face to the Baal Shem Tov and smiled at him. The Baal Shem Tov lifted the boy up into the air, above the heads of the people and smiled the biggest, broadest, happiest smile anyone had ever seen. And he called out, "This is our *T'kiah G'dolah!* This is our proudest, most joyous call and prayer to God! Until now, I was not certain that God could hear our prayers. I could feel that God knew that not all of us were praying with all our hearts and might. But this shepherd boy saved us. His love for God, and his excitement over the prayers and the shofar helped God to hear our prayers!"

From that day forward, the boy and the Baal Shem Tov began to meet early every morning, before it was time to take out the sheep. The Baal Shem Tov taught the boy Hebrew and the boy taught the Baal Shem Tov how to sing with the flute.

God heard everyone's prayer.

Answer Two: Rabbi Joshua Hammerman

God Understands All Languages

God understands all languages equally well, including sign language and body language—even computer language. No matter how we communicate, when people make connections, God is there.

Hebrew is a special language for the Jews. It helps us to experience God best because it connects us to other Jewish people—in the past, in the present and in the future—all over the world. Hebrew links us to our own grandparents and great-grandparents, many of whom prayed the same exact prayers in Hebrew that we pray. It also makes a link with the State of Israel, our homeland, and all who live there.

Most of all, when we use Hebrew it connects us to Hebrew. Hebrew letters are so old that they are among the first ways that people ever wrote down words. We can see these ancient letters on old coins and in museums. At the same time, Hebrew is so modern that it can spell Coca-Cola and so ancient that it takes us back to the beginnings of civilization. It is a very special language indeed.

Hebrew brings us closer to God because it helps us to connect to so many other people and to ourselves.

Answer Three:
Rabbi Brad Artson

Hebrew Works in Buenos Aires

The reason we pray in Hebrew is to connect to God and other Jews. If we each prayed in our local languages, then a Jew from Buenos Aires could not pray in a synagogue in Montreal, and a Jew from London could not pray with a congregation in Tel Aviv. By working hard to learn Hebrew, we maintain our precious link to the language of the Bible and the language of the Jewish people worldwide.

Hebrew connects all Jews.

Answer Four:
Joel Lurie Grishaver

The Golem

When God was ready to create the world, God used the Torah as a blueprint. Using the Hebrew words of the Torah, God created the world and everything in it. People were the last thing that God created. God shaped Adam out of the earth and breathed the breath of life into him with the help of Hebrew letters. Every language has power—the words of any tongue can create or destroy—but Hebrew has special powers.

Once, long ago in Prague, the Jews were in lots of trouble. Some of the non-Jews of Prague accused them of doing bad things, including killing Christian children. People believed these lies, and it looked as though there would be a big riot. Rabbi Judah Low was the leader of the Jewish community. He knew many of the secrets of the Hebrew language, including some of the Hebrew words God had used to create the world.

One night at midnight, Rabbi Low went to the banks of the river. He dug up some mud and used it to sculpt a giant human shape. Then he said prayers and combinations of Hebrew words and letters, including the words God used to create the world. Rabbi Low wrote three letters on the mud-man's head—*Alef*, the first letter in the *Alef-Bet*; *Mem*, the middle letter; and *Tav*, the last letter. The three letters spelled *emet*, the Hebrew word for truth. It is also one of God's names. The mud came to life as a giant called the Golem.

The Golem was like a person, but he could not speak or decide on his own what to do. At night, he patrolled the streets of the Jewish ghetto and kept everyone safe. During the day, the Golem worked for Rabbi Low. Eventually, the Golem became a detective to find out who was spreading lies about the Jews and, at the last moment, was able to stop a plot against the Jews and save the community. When the Golem's work was done, Rabbi Low said more Hebrew prayers, words and combinations of letters. He erased the *Alef* on the Golem's forehead. The Golem was again just a pile of mud. Without the *Alef*, all that was left was the Hebrew word *met*, which means death. Without the *Alef*, the Golem died.

Hebrew is very powerful; it is the language God used to create the world.

Your Turn

Each of our teachers answered the question "Does God understand Hebrew best?" in a different way.

 Rabbi Frishman told **The Story of the Flute.** It is the story of a boy who didn't know the words to the prayers but who played music with deep feeling. This story teaches us that God cares more about our feelings than about our words—in any language.

 Rabbi Hammerman said that God understands all languages but Hebrew connects Jews to their history.

 Rabbi Artson also said that God understands all languages, but Hebrew is very old and connects us to all Jews who have ever lived.

 Joel Grishaver told the story of the Golem. In this story, a rabbi used the same Hebrew words that God used to create the world to create a living thing that saved the Jewish community. This story teaches that Hebrew has powers beyond those of any other language.

Do you like any of these answers to the question? Is one of them close to your answer? Do you have a different answer?

The Prayers of Your Heart

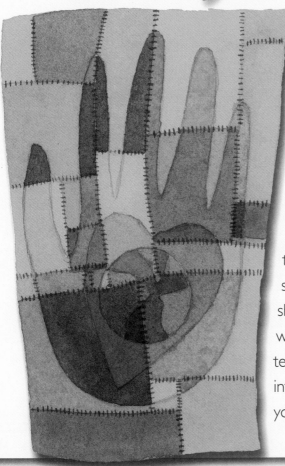

There is another <u>H</u>asidic story that is very much like the one that Rabbi Frishman told.

This story also starts with a shepherd boy who did not have time to go to school and could not read. All the boy knew were the letters of the Hebrew *Alef-Bet*. Just like the boy in the other story, this boy went to Yom Kippur services with his father. His heart, too, was moved by the beauty of the prayers and the songs. This boy had no flute and could not share his feelings with music. Instead, the boy shouted out, *"Alef, Bet, Gimmel, Dalet!"* Then he whispered, "God, all I know are Hebrew letters. Please put them together to make them into the words and the prayers that will move your heart."

Take these letters and arrange them into prayers.

1. H S E A M   R Y I L S E A   Ş _ _ _ _   _ _ _ _ _ _ _

2. D I K H U S D   _ _ _ _ _ _ _ _

3. A H Z M T O I   _ _ - _ _ _ _ _

4. U A R B H K E   _ _ _ _ _ _ _

5. H E E E S H Y U N A <u>H</u>   _ _ _ _ _ _ _ _ _ _ _

A Hebrew Secret

Many American Jews don't understand the meaning of Hebrew words. So why is Hebrew important?

Well, Hebrew is kind of magical. Hebrew words—and even Hebrew letters—have secrets that other languages don't have. For example, check out the letter פ *Peh*. Now, if you look very carefully inside this letter, you will see another Hebrew letter formed by the white space. It is the letter ב *Bet*.

When a scribe writes a Torah scroll, the פ *Peh* must always be written so that the ב *Bet* is there. Why?

Here is what Rabbi Gedalia Druin, a scribe, once taught me. He said, the letter פ *Peh* means "mouth." And the letter ב *Bet* is the first letter of the Torah, the beginning of the word בְּרֵאשִׁית *Bereshit*. Having the ב *Bet* inside the פ *Peh* reminds us that whenever words come out of our mouth, out of our פ *Peh*, they should be words of Torah. I think that's pretty cool. **Rabbi Elyse Frishman**

Here is the Hebrew *Alef-Bet*. Can you find another letter with a secret message? Use your imagination and find another message in the shape of one of the letters.

א ב ב ג ד ה ו ז ח ט י כ כ ד ל
מ ם נ ן ס ע פ פ ף צ ץ ק ר ש ש ת

_____

_____

Is the Bible True?

Answer One: Rabbi Jeff Salkin

Shelley Roff's Story is a Bible Story

Here is one example of how the Bible is true.

The early childhood director at our synagogue, Shelley Roff, told me this story about her family. It seems that her grandfather fled from Russia near the beginning of the twentieth century. The Russian army used to draft Jewish boys, which was just an easy way to make sure that those boys would be lost to the Jewish community and Judaism. They took these boys away from home when they were very young and kept them away for a long time. Most of them never found their way home again. Home was too far away and too long ago for them to know the way back.

Shelley's family paid for a poor boy to take her grandfather's place in the draft.

On the first night of Pesa<u>h</u>, during the Seder, a neighbor came to their house and warned her grandfather that the police had discovered the trick, and that they were coming to take him away. It was right in the middle of the Seder, but the young man got up, left the house, and escaped from Russia, leaving the rest of his family to finish the Seder.

Shelley told me that, to this day her family stops its Seder right at the point where her grandfather left his Seder and Russia! And they remember.

Is the story of the Exodus from Egypt true? You bet. Maybe it did not happen exactly the way it says in the Bible or in the exact way that we tell the story in the Haggadah. But the story is true! We know it is true because a miracle helped Shelley's grandfather leave a land of slavery and come to a place of freedom. Just like the Jews of Egypt, he was saved by a miraculous warning and had to leave in the middle of the night—Seder night—without even having time to "let the matzah rise." Whenever we remember how precious freedom is to us, it helps us to remember that the Bible is true.

Answer Two: Rabbi Ed Feinstein

Adam and Eve Teach Us That All People Are One Family

The Bible is a book written down long ago by the wisest of Jewish teachers to show us how to live the very best life we can. It tells us how to live a life of goodness, of caring, of happiness, of peace.

The Bible tells us that we all come from Adam and Eve. Is this really true? No one knows. The facts of the story may or may not be true. But the idea of the story is very true: If we all came from the same mom and dad, that makes us all family. And being family makes us all responsible for one another. That story tells me that I'm responsible even for people who look differently than I do, who speak different languages, who worship God differently, who live far away—they are all my brothers and sisters, and I'm responsible for them all.

The Bible is true if we learn to live according to its lessons.

Answer Three: Rabbi Elyse Frishman

The Bible is Like a Magic Eye Trick

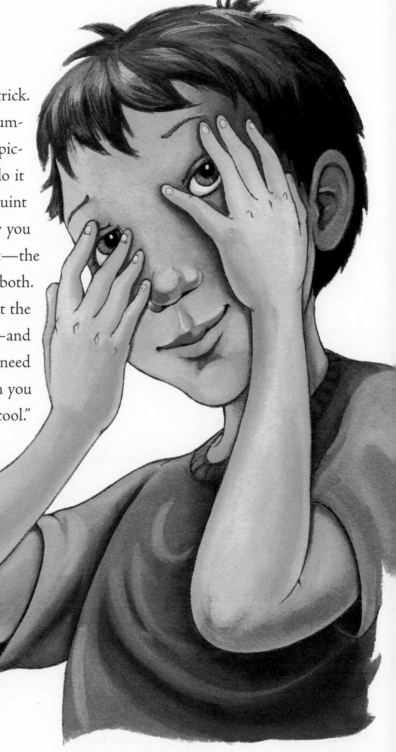

The Bible is like a magic eye trick. At first glance, there's this jumbled up picture. Is it really a jumbled up picture? Well, yes and no. If you learn to do it properly, you can close your eyes and squint at the Bible a certain way, and suddenly you see a whole new picture. So which is it—the jumble or the hidden picture? Well, it's both. Some people will never be able to squint the right way and will only see the jumble—and they will say, "This is stupid. I don't need this," and they will walk away. But when you see the hidden picture, you say, "This is cool." That is what the Bible is like to me.

Does it matter to me if everything in the Bible happened exactly the way it says? No, because I am more interested in the other hidden meanings.

Your Turn

All three of our rabbis believe the Bible is true. Are you surprised? The interesting part is the different ways that they believe that the Bible is true. Although there are rabbis who will say that God told every single word of the Bible to Moses on the top of Mt. Sinai, none of our rabbis did. Does that surprise you?

 Rabbi Jeff Salkin told us **Shelley Roff's Story is a Bible Story.** Her grandfather was rescued on Passover night in the same way that the Jewish people were rescued on the same night. Rabbi Salkin explained that the Bible is true because its stories come true in different ways in each of our lives.

 Rabbi Ed Feinstein said, "The Bible is a book written down long ago by the wisest of Jewish teachers." He pointed out that the story of **Adam and Eve Teaches Us That All People Are One Family.** He added, "The Bible is true if we learn to live according to its lessons."

 Rabbi Elyse Frishman taught that **The Bible is Like a Magic Eye Trick.** She teaches that there are things to see in the Torah that are deeper than the story and that the truth of the Torah is in the hidden meanings.

Which of these understandings of the Bible is closest to yours?
How do you answer the question, "Is the Torah true?"

Tanakh = Bible

The Bible is a lot like a library. It is not one book, but rather a collection of thirty-nine books. These books are divided into three big sections.

תּוֹרָה **The Torah** contains the Five Books of Moses. The Torah starts with the creation of the world and ends with the death of Moses.

נְבִיאִים **The Prophets** comes next. The Prophets continue the story. They start with the Families-of-Israel leaving the wilderness and entering the Land of Israel. A prophet is a person who brings us a lesson from God. Many of the stories in The Prophets teach us to think about the way we are acting and change our behavior.

כְּתוּבִים **The Writings** are all the other books in the Bible. Some of them are poetry. Some of them are individual stories. Still others are wise things to know.

תַּנַ"ךְ **Tanakh** is the Hebrew name for the Bible. It is made up of *Torah*, *Nivi'im*, and *K'tuvim*.

Bible Hunt

Torah

Prophets

Writings

You will need a *Tanakh* to do this activity. Look up each of the following books and write down the section of the Bible in which it is found: Torah, Prophets or Writings.

1. Esther _____

2. Deuteronomy _____

3. Isaiah _____

4. Ruth _____

5. Exodus _____

6. Samuel _____

Your Bible Stories

Rabbi Shneur Zalman was thrown in jail unfairly. He taught a Bible lesson to his cruel jail guard. He asked the guard, "Do you remember the question that God asked Adam and Eve in the Garden of Eden?" The guard knew the answer and said, "God asked them, 'Where are you?'" The rabbi then said to the guard, "God is asking you the same question. 'Where are you? What are you doing right now?'" The guard thought about the rabbi's words, thought about his life and changed at that very moment. He became kind rather than remaining cruel.

Rabbi Shneur Zalman taught that the stories in the Torah are always true. They happen over and over again. Every person can find his or her own story in the Torah.

Being a Bible Person

Answer at least one of these questions.

1. When all of the other brothers were ready to kill Joseph, his brother Reuben stepped in and saved his life. When have you been like Reuben and tried to make peace in a family?

2. Ruth was a very loyal friend. Because of her friendship with Naomi, she left her home and went to Israel. When have you been like Ruth, a very loyal person who did something difficult to help a friend?

3. Esther was a very brave woman. When the Jewish people were being attacked, she risked her life to make sure that they were safe. When have you been like Esther and worked hard to keep other people safe?

4. Nathan was a prophet who risked his life by telling King David that he had done the wrong thing. When have you been like Nathan, taking a risk to make sure that justice happened?

_____

_____

Does God Really Make Miracles?

Answer One: Joel Lurie Grishaver

Some Miracles We Don't Know About

In the Talmud they tell this story. Two men began a long trip. The first leg of the journey was to walk from their town to the harbor. From there they were going to take a boat across the sea. The two men started to walk, when one of them stepped on a thorn and had to stop to see a doctor. The wound hurt a lot and the men missed their boat. One of the men began to yell at God. He asked, "Why are you punishing me?" A few days later, the two men learned that there had been an accident at sea. The boat on which they would have sailed sank. Everyone on it was lost. The two men started to praise God. For them the thorn was a miracle.

Recently a woman told me a similar story. Her grandmother came from Eastern Europe to New York. She moved in with her brother and the first thing he told her was that to stay in his house she needed a job. She agreed. Then he told her that her work started the following day—he had already found her a job. She said, "But tomorrow is Shabbat and I can't work on Shabbat." He said, "If you want to live in my house, you will have to work when the work is there." The next morning she got up and pretended to go to work. She spent all day hiding. She did not stay home, but she did not go to work either.

After sunset, when the workday was over, she went home. When she opened the door, the living room was filled people screaming and crying. Clearly, something was wrong. When she asked what was going on, everyone turned to look at her in shock. Some screamed. Some almost fainted. She was told that the Triangle Shirtwaist Factory, where she was supposed to work, had burned down that day.

The Triangle Shirtwaist Factory fire is very famous. On March 26, 1911, 141 people, mostly young women, were burned to death. Once the fire started, there was no way out of the factory.

For this woman and her family, that Shabbat was a miracle.

In the Talmud (Niddah 31a) we are told, "Not even the person for whom a miracle was made always knows that a miracle has happened." Our world is filled with miracles. One of our jobs is to recognize them.

Answer Two: Rabbi Josh Hammerman and Rabbi Brad Artson

"Oh My God" Moments

What is a miracle? I would define a miracle as something that makes someone say, "Oh, my God!" Therefore, for me, miracles have something to do with God. Some miracles are made by God alone (for instance, a spectacular sunset), but the best miracles require the cooperation of people—things like the creation of a new baby or a new country. Israel was the answer to the prayers of many generations, but it would never have been established without much human sacrifice. So think of all the times you are so overcome that you just have to say, "Oh, my God!" Most likely, you are witnessing a miracle.

Rabbi Joshua Hammerman

God makes miracles all the time. In fact, God's miracles are so frequent and so numerous that we've stopped noticing them. Did you see the sun come up this morning? Wasn't that magnificent! And you can count on it coming up again tomorrow and the day after and the day after that. Did you notice how unbelievably cool it is that a collection of organic chemical compounds (me) can write down thoughts in words and a second collection of organic compounds (you) can read those words and share my thoughts? Have you stopped to think how incredible it is that there are Jews today, after thousands of years of wandering, with no army or nation of our own for most of our history? All we had was the Torah and our faith, yet here we are. And the mighty nations that tried to kill us with powerful armies—they're the ones who are gone! Or think about how incredible it is that we already find yesterday's papers and last month's magazines boring, yet the Torah and Talmud are millennia old and still incredibly relevant! Does God make miracles? Just look around!

Rabbi Brad Artson

Answer Three: Rabbi Ed Feinstein

I Was Sick and Then I Got Better

This year, I was very sick with a disease called cancer. I got better. To my doctor, this was nothing special—just the result of good medicine. But to me and to my family, it was a miracle. I got my life back. I got to be with my family and my friends. It was the best present I've ever received.

A miracle isn't something that breaks the rules of nature. It can be perfectly natural and still be a miracle. A miracle is an event that changes our lives—opening up a new future for us. The Hebrew word for miracle is נֵס *nes*—which really means "sign." A miracle is an event that gives us a sign that we can have hope. A miracle is a sign that our dreams of making a better world might actually come true.

A miracle is a sign that God cares for us.

Your Turn

Our teachers gave us lots of different answers to the question, "Does God really make miracles?"

Joel Grishaver said, **"Some Miracles We Don't Know About."** He told the story of the woman who was saved from the Triangle Shirtwaist Factory fire because she would not work on Shabbat. He quoted the Talmud that teaches, "Not even the person for whom a miracle was made always knows that the miracle has happened."

Rabbi Josh Hammerman talked about **"Oh, My God"** moments and Rabbi Brad Artson said, "God's miracles are so frequent and so numerous that we've stopped noticing them." Both of them say that our lives are filled with miracles—ordinary miracles.

Rabbi Ed Feinstein told the story of his recovery from cancer. He said, **"I Was Sick and Then I Got Better."** That was a miracle for him and his family. He tells that a miracle is a sign that God cares for us.

Is your understanding of miracles close to one of these understandings?
Do you have a different understanding of miracles? What is it?

A Shoebox Full of Miracles

Most families have a book, a shoebox or a drawer filled with family photographs. Today, some families keep their photographs on disk or CD-ROM. Family photographs tell the story of vacations and sporting events, of weddings and b'nai mitzvah, of Thanksgiving dinners and ordinary moments. When we take and save family photographs, we are collecting experiences we want to remember.

The rabbis of the Talmud invented a different way of storing memories. They created a memory *brakhah* (blessing). This blessing is the *Sheheheyanu*. It thanks God for special moments.

בָּרוּךְ אַתָּה יי אֱלֹהֵינוּ מֶלֶךְ הָעוֹלָם שֶׁהֶחֱיָנוּ וְקִיְּמָנוּ וְהִגִּיעָנוּ לַזְּמַן הַזֶּה.

Barukh Attah Adonai Eloheinu Melekh ha-Olam
she-he-he'yanu v'ki'y'manu v'higi'anu la-z'man ha-zeh.

Praise are You, The Eternal, Ruler of the Cosmos, Who keeps us alive, and Who keeps us going, and Who helps us reach this time.

List three Sheheheyanu moments that are ordinary miracles you want to remember always.

1. _____

2. _____

3. _____

The Big Miracles

In Pirke Avot we are told that on the first Friday, in the last few minutes before the first Shabbat, God created ten major miracles. God spent all week creating the ordinary miracles, then in the last few minutes, God created a few extraordinary ones.

If you were God, what ten miracles, starting with Adam and Eve, would you pick to wind up with a perfect world?

1. _____
2. _____
3. _____
4. _____
5. _____
6. _____
7. _____
8. _____
9. _____
10. _____

The Big Miracles

This is the list of ten miracles found in Pirke Avot.

Ten things were created on the eve of the first Shabbat, just before the first candle lighting:

[1] The mouth of the earth *that swallowed Korah, a rebel who tried to take over and kick out Moses, and his cohorts.*

[2] The mouth of Miriam's well *that moved through the wilderness so that the families of Israel always had water.*

[3] The mouth of the donkey *that spoke to Bilaam.*

[4] The rainbow *that appeared at the end of the flood.*

[5] The manna *that the families of Israel ate in the wilderness.*

[6] The staff *that Moses used to make many other miracles. It may originally have belonged to Adam.*

[7] The Shamir, *a miraculous worm that cut the stones for Solomon's Temple so that no metal was needed. Metal is used to make the weapons that kill people.*

[8] The writing tool *that cut the words into the two Tablets.*

[9] The letters of the first commandments *that could be read correctly from both sides.*

[10] The tablets of stone *for the first set of commandments.*

Some people add Moses' grave, the ram, and the tongs that made the very first pair of tongs. (5.6)

Discussion Questions: Which miracles are the strangest? Which miracles are on the list that you made? Do any of them need an explanation? Do you believe that the big miracles in the Bible really happened? Why do you think that miracles like that don't happen any more? How did your list of ten miracles compare to the list found in Pirke Avot?

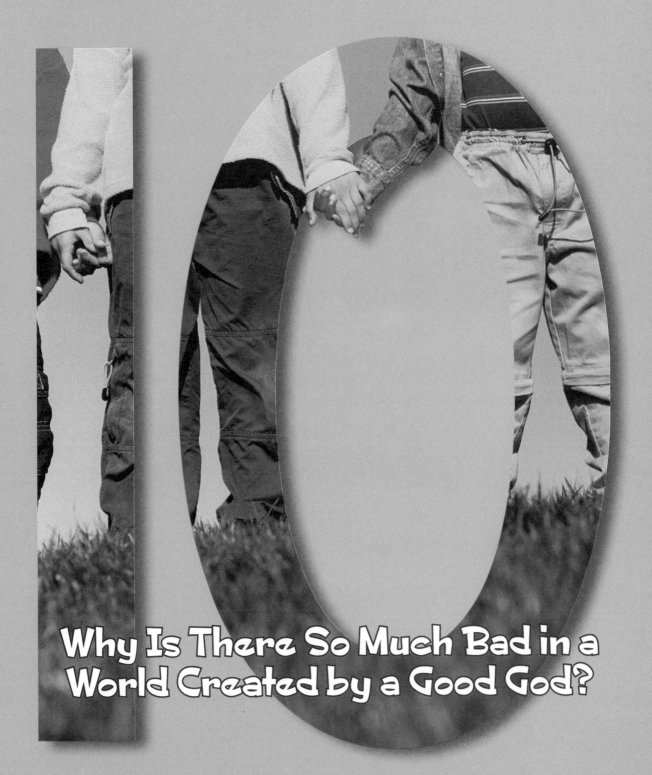

Why Is There So Much Bad in a World Created by a Good God?

Answer One: Rabbi Jeff Salkin

God's Letter to Peter

I once read a book called *Children's Letters to God*. These are real letters that kids have written. Here is one of my favorites:

Dear God,

Please send Donald Epstein to a different camp next year.

Peter

This is how I imagine God might have answered Peter's letter:

Dear Peter,

I am sorry about your concern regarding the matter of Donald Epstein. Why don't you like Donald Epstein? I imagine that it is because you don't get along. Maybe Donald short-sheeted your bed. Maybe he hit you with water balloons in a late night raid on your bunk. I know about pests. Ever since Cain and Abel I know about people who don't get along.

First of all, I have to tell you something about Me and the way that I work. I don't know what people have been telling you, but despite what a lot of people think, I really don't have that much control over people and what they do.

Take the word that you used: "send." The question is, Do I, as God, send anyone anywhere? Well, I guess you could say that I sent Abraham to Canaan, and that I sent Moses to Pharaoh, and that I sent the prophets on their missions. The big point here is that those people felt that they were on a mission from Me. That means that they had a holy task to do. I don't send people places, but sometimes when they get to where they're going, they realize that they have gone there for a holy purpose, and so they think that I sent them. That's okay with Me. But I'm afraid that I can't send Donald Epstein to another camp next summer.

Why not, you might ask? Because sending Donald Epstein to camp is what his parents are supposed to do. That's their job. Now, I really can't go around stopping parents from sending their kids to a certain camp, just because one kid doesn't like another. I can't, and I won't. If I had the power to make parents send their kids to certain camps, then I would have the power to send anyone anywhere. This means that I could have easily used that power to send Adolph Hitler to be a painter in Antarctica so he would never have hurt anyone. I would stop people from doing drugs and abusing alcohol.

I just can't do it. I made people free to make their own decisions. Sometimes, quite often to be honest with you, they make terrible decisions that really hurt them and other people. But I can't stop them from doing that, because then I wouldn't have free and responsible people in my world.

So, I'm afraid you're stuck with the real possibility that Mr. and Mrs. Epstein are going to send Donald back to your camp. That's just the way it goes. If I had the power to make people do only what I want, then I would have used that power a long time ago. But I made people free, and ever since then, the world has had to live with that.

If Donald Epstein comes back to camp next summer and he makes your life miserable, I will feel terrible for you. I will know how you feel. Whenever people mistreat each other, I feel terrible. I wish I could stop it, but I can't.

Here's what I can do. I can try to give you the strength to cope with Donald Epstein next summer. Try this prayer: "O God, give me the strength to cope with Donald Epstein. I realize that he might do some bad things to me. Give me the strength to tolerate him, to stand up to him, maybe even to fight back or to go to a counselor and say, 'Tell Donald Epstein to cut me some slack.' Blessed are You, O God, Who gives strength to the weary."

One last thing. There is a very good possibility that Donald Epstein will change over the next year. If he was mean last summer, maybe he will get nicer. I help people change and grow. And I help people learn to live even with those who cannot change and grow.

Thanks for writing.

Love forever, God.

God wants people to be good. God gave the mitzvot to the Jewish people to help them become good. But God cannot force people to be good. God made people free to live their lives the way they want. This means that people are free to be as good or as bad as they want to be.

Imagine how God feels about this. There is an ancient legend that says that there is a secret room in the heavens where God goes to cry. God cries because of all the terrible things that people do to each other. And God also cries because God can't stop it. To do so would mean taking away people's ability to make their own choices.

Answer Two: Rabbi Sybil Sheridan

We are Not Robots

When the world was created, God could have made robots instead of people. They would have been neither good nor bad, just programmed. But to make the world very good, God needed people who wanted to make it even better. Unfortunately, once you can <u>want</u> to do good, you can also <u>want</u> to do bad things, and many people did just that.

God could step in and sort it all out, but instead God made us partners and it is our job to make the world the best it can be.

97

Answer Three: Rabbi Ed Feinstein

We Are a Little Like God and a Little Like the Animals

When God designed people, we were made a little like God and a little like the animals. Like God, we can think and talk and create, we can love and care and dream of a better world. Like animals, we get angry, we hurt others, we can even kill. We're a combination and we are given the ability to choose which part of ourselves we'd like to follow. When people choose to be like God, they bring goodness to the world. But people can also choose to be like animals. They can choose to hurt, to steal, to kill, to be selfish and mean. At the very beginning, God decided not to interfere when people make a choice. It hurts God when we choose to be animals and mess up the world, but God won't stop us. That's our choice. We must live with the consequences of that choice. Each time we choose to be like God—making peace, healing the sick, feeding the hungry—God celebrates with us.

98

Your Turn

In this chapter we asked the question, "Why is there so much bad in a world created by a good God?" All three of our rabbis gave more or less the same answer in a different way. Each of them talked about "free will."

Rabbi Jeff Salkin wrote a letter from God to Peter explaining that prayers have nothing to do with whether or not Donald Epstein will return to camp. Rabbi Salkin has God say, "I don't work that way." He says God cannot force people to be good. Rabbi Salkin says that God says, "I made people free to make their own decisions."

Rabbi Sybil Sheridan explains that God made people not robots. We have to make the right choices. She explains, "God made us partners instead and it is our job to make the world the best it can be."

Rabbi Ed Feinstein explains that we are a little like God and a little like the animals. When people choose to be like God, they bring goodness to the world. But people can also choose to be like animals. They can choose to hurt, to steal, to kill, to be selfish and mean.

All of the rabbis explained that bad things come into the world because God gave us the ability to choose. Do you agree? Each of the rabbis explained this choice in a different way. Is one of the explanations close to what you believe?

Do you have another way of understanding this?

A Letter from God

Rabbi Salkin wrote a letter from God to Peter in order to explain what he believed about God. Write a letter from God to <u>H</u>annah to explain your thoughts about God.

Dear God,

We had an earthquake yesterday and I got very scared. Sometimes when there are earthquakes people get hurt. Why didn't you make a better world that didn't have storms and volcanos and earthquakes and other things that scare and hurt people?

Hannah

Dear <u>H</u>annah,

_____

_____

_____

_____

_____

_____

God

A Hidden Message

Here is a sentence from the Torah that is part of the worship service. The Torah says,

וְאָהַבְתָּ אֵת יי אֱלֹהֶיךָ בְּכָל-לְבָבְךָ וּבְכָל-נַפְשְׁךָ וּבְכָל-מְאֹדֶךָ

And you shall love the Eternal your God, with all your heart, with all your soul and with all your might.

The rabbis of the Talmud explained that there is a secret message hidden in the word

L'vav'kha .... לְבָבְךָ (With all your heart)

Here is the clue to the secret. The usual word for heart is לֵב *lev* with one ב *Vet*. לְבָבְךָ *L'vav'kha* has two *Vet* letters. (Can you circle them?) The Talmud explains that the two *Vet* letters stand for the two sides of your heart, the animal side and the Godlike side. We are commanded to love God with all of our heart—that means both the animal side and the Godlike side. It then explains that the secret to loving God is to use our animal side to do holy things.

what holy thing can you do with...

the desire to be powerful?

_____

the desire to have the most?

_____

a love of eating?

_____

the ability to get angry?

_____

Does God Punish People?

Answer One: Rabbi
Ed Feinstein

The Story of Berel and Shmerel

Berel and Shmerel were among those who left Egypt. As slaves, they had grown so accustomed to looking down at the ground that they could no longer lift their eyes. And so when Moses brought us across the Red Sea, and all of Israel witnessed the great miracle, Berel asked Shmerel, "What do you see?"

"I see mud," Shmerel responded.

"I see mud too. What's all this about freedom? We had mud in Egypt, we have mud here!"

When we stood at Mt. Sinai in God's presence and heard the voice of God, Shmerel asked Berel, "What do you hear?"

"I hear someone shouting commands," Berel answered.

"I hear commands, too. What's all this about Torah? They shouted commands in Egypt. They shout commands here!"

Finally, after forty years, when we arrived at the Promised Land, the land of milk and honey, Berel asked Shmerel, "How do you feel?"

"My feet hurt," Shmerel replied.

"My feet hurt, too. What's all this about a Promised Land? My feet hurt in Egypt. My feet hurt here!"

So what did they do? They turned around and went back. Some say that Berel and Shmerel are still wandering around the wilderness. Others say they returned to Egypt—back to the Pharaoh, back to being slaves—because they couldn't lift their eyes to see the miracles all around them.

When we do the wrong thing, most of the time it isn't because we've become evil or rejected good. Most of the time, we do the wrong thing because we're not paying attention. We forget who we are, who we're with and what we've been asked to do in the world. We forget to lift up our eyes and we miss the miracles all around us. That's the reason we do the wrong thing—and it's also our punishment. When we do the wrong thing, God doesn't throw down lightning from the sky. That's not how God operates. When we do right, it's as if we're moving ourselves and the whole world closer to the Promised Land. But when we do wrong, it's as if we're moving backward on the journey—back toward Egypt. Egypt is the place where people are turned into objects and objects are worshiped as if they were God. Just ask Berel and Shmerel...if you can find them!

Answer Two: Rabbi Sybil Sheridan
and Rabbi Brad Artson

People Punish Themselves

If you stole the last cookies in the jar, there might not be any cookies next time you looked, or you might end up with a pain or being sick. Your mum might find out and punish you; she might remove the cookie jar so you could never get at it again. She might stop buying cookies altogether. Above all, you would carry inside of you a feeling of guilt, which would spoil the taste. God doesn't need to punish people, they seem very able to punish themselves.

Sybil Sheridan

Our Actions Have Consequences

When a good parent punishes a child, the purpose of the punishment is to help the child learn to do right in the future. An effective punishment is a teaching tool. It helps us to learn that there are consequences to wrongdoing. When we do something wrong, there are usually consequences in the long run. God's "punishments" are simply the consequences of our wrongdoing. If we give way to our selfishness and greed, then we'll all drive in our private cars, and our skies will get polluted, and our highways will be clogged. Those aren't punishments to make us suffer, but consequences to encourage us to be responsible and good.

Rabbi Brad Artson

Answer Three: Rabbi Jeff Salkin

God Rewards and Punishes People in the World-to-Come

Sometimes, evil people are punished in this life. For example, if they are lawbreakers, they may get arrested and get put in jail. Here, a human judge imitates the actions of the Divine Judge. But sometimes, the punishment for evil people is very quiet and almost invisible. Their reputations are ruined. They lose their friends and the love of their family. People no longer trust them. They wind up with "uckiness" inside them that does not go away. And if they have any conscience at all, their conscience may bother them terribly.

But not everyone gets their due reward in this life. Good people do not always get what they deserve and bad people do not always get what they deserve either. That is why the answer to this question is very important. When good people have painful lives, God rewards them the world-to-come—the world that comes after death. When bad people have joyous lives, God punishes them in the world-to-come. We cannot understand exactly how this happens and we will never understand it. But that's the nice thing about faith; it gives us a way of being "sure" about something for which we cannot have scientific proof.

Your Turn

Our rabbis gave us very different answers to the question "Does God punish people?"
Rabbi Feinstein told **The Story of Berel and Shmerel.** These were two Jews who left

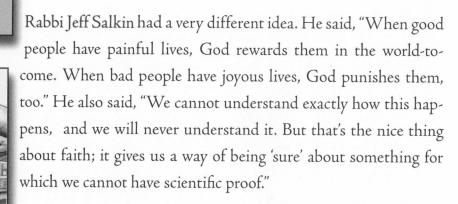

Egypt and saw all the miracles as punishments because they looked at their feet rather than looking around. Rabbi Feinstein says, "When we do the wrong thing, God doesn't throw down lightning from the sky...when we do wrong, it's as if we're moving backward on the journey—back toward Egypt."

Rabbi Sybil Sheridan talked about a cookie jar. She explained that people punish themselves. Rabbi Brad Artson agreed with her and added that our actions have consequences. Both rabbis agree that, "When we do something wrong there are usually consequences in the long run. God's 'punishments' are simply the consequences of our wrongdoing."

Rabbi Jeff Salkin had a very different idea. He said, "When good people have painful lives, God rewards them in the world-to-come. When bad people have joyous lives, God punishes them, too." He also said, "We cannot understand exactly how this happens, and we will never understand it. But that's the nice thing about faith; it gives us a way of being 'sure' about something for which we cannot have scientific proof."

**Is one of these answers close to your answer to the question?
Do you have a different way of explaining how good people are
rewarded
and bad people are punished?**

GOOD PUNISHMENT/
BAD PUNISHMENT

What are three things that make a punishment a good punishment?

1. _____

2. _____

3. _____

What are three things that make a punishment a bad punishment?

1. _____

_____

2. _____

_____

3. _____

_____

What is the worst punishment that you ever got? _____

_____

What is the best punishment that you ever got? _____

_____

T'shuvah

Here is a story from the Talmud:

Rabbi Simeon ben Lakish was a thief before he became a rabbi. He was part of a three-man gang. Although Rabbi Simeon changed and became a much better person, his two partners in crime did not change. It happened that all three of the men died on the same day. Rabbi Simeon was taken to *Gan Eden* ("the Jewish heaven"). The other two went to *Gehinom* ("the Jewish other place"). The two men in *Gehinom* complained to God, "All three of us did the same crimes—how come we got punished and he got rewarded?" God said to them, "Rabbi Simeon did *t'shuvah* | (repentence) and you did not."

What do you think this story means?

What is t'shuvah (repentence)?
T'shuvah is...

- admitting that what you have done is wrong
- asking forgiveness of the person you hurt and of God
- fixing what ever you broke (including feelings)
- doing the inner-work necessary for you to change, so that this problem will never be repeated

1. Which part of this process is the hardest to do?
2. Which part of this process is the easiest to do?
3. Can you feel a difference when you make *t'shuvah*?

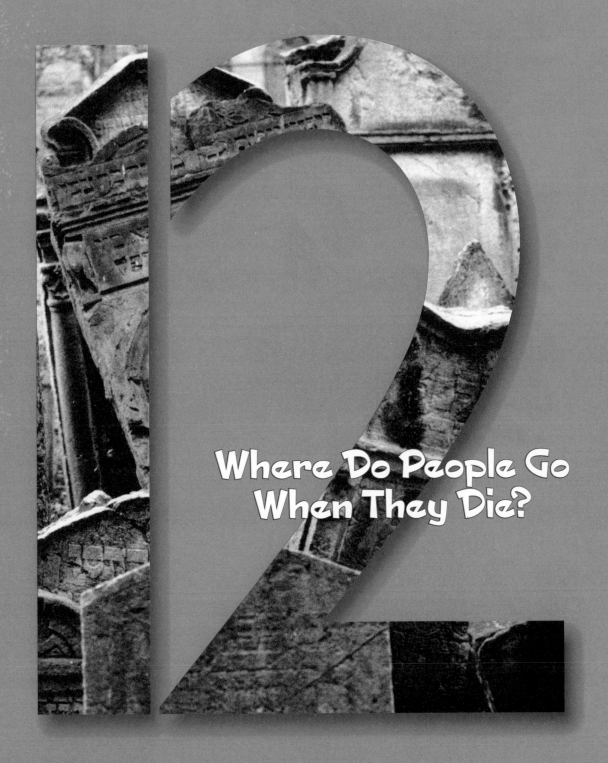

12

Where Do People Go
When They Die?

Answer One: Rabbi Joshua Hammerman

People Live On in the Good Things That They Did

When you shout into an echoing canyon and your voice comes back at you, at first loud and clear and then less so, what happens to it in the end? Does it continue to bounce back and forth forever, just a little softer each time? In some ways, our lives are like that. Except that once we've shouted into the canyon, because we've poured all our love and our tears into that one cry, the echo doesn't necessarily get softer with the passing of time. Sometimes the echo gets louder over the years. Look at Moses' echo!

Sometimes a person's life appears to be forgotten forever, but then a ripple effect is felt, in some form, generations later.

My father died twenty years ago, when I was a young man. Recently, I discovered his name on the Internet! A person I had never met was paying tribute to my dad on a Website. When I happened to read that tribute, it was as if my father had come back to life. My father was a cantor and a very public person who did lots of nice things for people. But even people who aren't well known can live on through their deeds. Here's a good example:

You may have heard of the story of Joseph from the book of Genesis. Joseph was Jacob's favorite son. Because of that, Joseph's brothers were extremely jealous of him. At one point, Jacob sent Joseph on a long journey to visit his brothers who were tending the family flocks. When Joseph arrived on the scene, his brothers threw him into a pit, then decided to sell him as a slave. The rest, as they say, is history. Joseph was taken to Egypt, where he eventually rose to the second highest office in the land, saving the Egyptian people—and his own family—from a seven-year famine. Years later, Jacob's entire family went down to Egypt to join Joseph. Eventually, the Israelites grew in number, were enslaved by the evil Pharaoh and later were freed by God and given the Torah.

But I left out one key detail. You see, Joseph almost never made it to the place where his brothers were tending the sheep. He lost his way! The Torah tells us that a "man" (*ish* in Hebrew) gave him the correct directions, just in the nick of time. If it weren't for that man—whose name we never learn—and that one simple deed of giving directions, the rest of Jewish history would never have happened!

I often think of my life as a wave in the ocean: I'll try to make as big a splash as I can on the shore before becoming part of the ocean again after I die.

The ancient rabbis instructed us to live each day as if it were to be our last. To me that means that we should perform each deed as if that particular act were the one that will have the most lasting impact on the world long after we are gone. For above all, Judaism tells us that our deeds define who we are and how we are to be remembered. The things we do in our lives, the things we say and the ways we show we care—these things live on, in some form, forever.

Answer Two: Rabbi Elyse Frishman

Our Souls Go Back to God

There is no way to know for sure where people go when they die because no one has ever come back to tell us the answer! Judaism teaches that when you die, your body becomes part of the earth again, but your soul lives forever and becomes part of God.

There is a very important idea in science that nothing can ever disappear. It always is around, in one form or another. The universe that God made a long time ago is still here today. Sure, stuff takes different forms—an ice cube can also be water or steam. Food gets used by the body and is turned into energy. But no thing ever disappears; it just changes into something else, kind of like animorphs or vegemorphs.

So when we die, our bodies turn back into dust. It takes a really, really long time, but that is what happens. What about the part of us that was our breath? What about our souls? Our soul is like a piece of God inside of us. When we die, that part becomes part of God again. Our bodies keep us separate from God just like they separate us from each other. But when our bodies are gone, nothing separates us, and our souls rush to become connected to God again.

Answer Three: Rabbi Sybil Sheridan

People Go Somewhere After This Life

I have seen people in the very last moments of an illness. Sometimes, when they die, a peaceful calm covers their faces, and sometimes they look as if they are smiling. Wherever they go, it seems to me, they are no longer sick, no longer suffering their terrible pain. They are not worried about anything any more. I can't tell you more about heaven than this, since I have never been there, but judging by the look on the faces of those who leave us, it must be a pretty amazing place.

Your Turn

This chapter was all about where people go when they die. There are five different major Jewish ideas about this. Three of our rabbis shared three of them.

Rabbi Joshua Hammerman said that people are remembered by the good things that they have done. He compared finding his father's name on the Internet to remembering the unnamed man who changed Jewish history by giving Joseph the directions he needed to find his brothers. Rabbi Hammerman said, "I often think of my life as a wave in the ocean: I'll try to make as big a splash as I can on the shore before becoming part of the ocean again after I die."

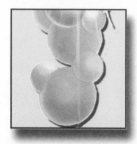

Rabbi Elyse Frishman said that our souls go back to God. She explains, "Our soul is like a piece of God inside of us, and when we die, that part becomes part of God again."

Rabbi Sybil Sheridan says that she believes that people go somewhere after this life. She says, "Sometimes, when they die, a peaceful calm covers their faces, and sometimes they look as if they are smiling. I can't tell you more about heaven than this, since I have never been there, but judging by the look on the faces of those who leave us, it must be a pretty amazing place."

Some Jews believe that when we die our soul leaves our body and becomes the soul of a newborn baby. This is called reincarnation.

Some Jews believe that after we die, we wait for the Messiah to come. When the time finally comes for God to help people make the world a perfect place, God will recreate our bodies and put our souls back into them. This is called "resurrection of the dead." It is an idea found in the traditional prayerbook.

What do you think?

Zakhor = Remembering

The Hebrew word *zakhor* means remembering. When people have died, Jews make a point of remembering them and remembering the things that they did. On the anniversary of their death we light a candle and remember. Four times a year we hold a special service called *Yizkor*. It is a service of remembering.

Who is one person you cared about who is no longer here?

_____

_____

_____

What is something you remember about her or him?

_____

_____

_____

I have some questions about God.

Three of my questions are:

1._____

2._____

3._____